For Marsha

Blessings & Butterflies!

Sandy Stillwell

POW WOW 2017

In A Dress

Made Of Butterflies

In A Dress

Made Of Butterflies

poems by

Sandra Lee Stillwell

Poetic Matrix Press
Madera, California

Cover Art
Legendary Spring Birds by David Chethlahe Paladin

I am forever indebted to Lynda Paladin not only for so graciously allowing me to use her late husband, David Chethlahe Paladin's artwork, but for choosing what I consider to be the perfect cover art for "In A Dress Made Of Butterflies." The caption under the photo she sent me reads: "Here's 'Legendary Spring Birds'. Although there are what look like butterflies, they are really winged serpents. This is about transition, from the old world that's dying to the new world that's being born...or created." It is a painting filled with hope. That is what I wanted my book to be.

Discovering "Painting The Dream", a beautiful book containing David Paladin's art and his story, was the first inspiration behind my need to write Native American poetry. It came to me in the early 1990's during a dark time when I was trying to find myself in the beginning of sobriety. I found his life story to be a strengthening tool to use along, what at times, was a difficult path. I was able to give away one addiction for another...poetry. I have not stopped.

Poetic Matrix Press
P.O. Box 1223
Madera, CA 93639
559.673.9402
www.poeticmatrix.com
poeticmatrix@yahoo.com

With Special Thanks To:

John Peterson, Publisher at Poetic Matrix Press and the On-line *periodic letteR*, for making this dream of a first book come true. James Downs for his editorial work, his friendship, his patience and willingness to work through the stubborn tenacious streak I have around my poems. Without his work and belief in me, many of these poems would not have made their way into this book. Dennis Noble, husband and friend, for his patience, his willingness to listen again and again to my poems as well as the poems of countless others, especially over the phone or just before we sleep and his willingness to travel with me wherever I have found a gathering of poets. My mother for the constant source of inspiration she is. My brother David for his computer expertise. Ila Berry, Claudia Moffitt, Susan Parker and Maria Rosales, for their encouragement and love. Joe Armstrong for his praise of my work, his willingness to print my poetry so often in *Hard Row To Hoe,* and for writing the beautiful heartfelt words for the back cover of the book. Sue Clark for insisting I learn the basics. Cheryl Dumesnil for insisting I tell her more and more still, and for her kind words on the back cover of the book. Diane Frank for teaching me the value of verbs.

I would like to thank Peter Bray for his kind words and encouragement. To Maria Rosales again, for founding Primo Poets and insisting I read my poems there. To all the poets who supported Primo Poets, sharing with me their love of poetry, their love for each other. And every poet near and far, who have made me feel warm and welcome in their many places of congregation. - Sandy

Acknowledgments:

•A Poem For Forest Deaner - *California Native Plant Society Newsletter.*
•A Train Travels Through His Poems - Grand Prize Winner, *Grandmother Earth VIII; Taproot and Aniseweed 2,* Peter Bray, Publisher.
•A Blossom Fully Opened - *Artscan,* Arts Council of The Napa Valley.
•About Jim Eagleheart's Flute - *White Pelican Review;* Honorable Mention Poet's Dinner, Berkeley California, 2003.
•At The Edge Of The Road - *Poetry Depth Quarterly.*
•Dead As Arthur's Tree - *Poetry Depth Quarterly.*
•Dry Creek Runs Wet In Winter - *Working Hard For The Money,* Bottom Dog Press.
•Earth Day 2004 - *Snowy Egret.*
•Eclipse - *Grandmother Earth VIII,* Honorable Mention.
•Egret - *Song Of The San Joaquin.*
•Grandmother's Slippers - *A&E,* Mendocino Art Council; *Sierra Nevada College Review; Soul Making Contest 2003* Honorable Mention.
•Great Grandmother - *Benicia Herald.*
•Here Among The Stones - *Erete's Bloom.*
•How Can I call You Dead? - *Tap Root and Aniseweed,* Peter Bray, publisher; *Women In The Arts 2004* Grand Prize Winner.
•Huntress - *Artscan; Poetry Depth Quarterly.*
•I sit, still myself - *ByLine; On-line periodic letteR -* Poetic Matrix Press; *Every First Tuesday* Anthology from Rock and Feather Press.
•In Raven's shadow - *The Third Sunday Group Anthology,* Richard Stella, Publisher; *Brevities; Helen Vaughn Johnson Memorial Haiku Award,* Honorable Mention; *Shared Haiku,* Women In The Arts.
•Kestrel At Dry Creek - *Poetry Depth Quarterly; The Gathering 8,* Ina Coolbrith Circle.
•Late In The Afternoon - *Artscan,* Arts Council Of The Napa Valley.

- My Neighbor Sleeps - *Hard Row To Hoe; Song Of The San Joaquin;* Honorable Mentions from The National League Of American Pen Women 41st Biennial Letters Competition 2002; *ByLine;* National League of American Pen Women Portland, Oregon; Soul Maker's Contest 2003.
- On Dusty Bookshelves - *ByLine.*
- Or So The Old Ones Say - *Hard Row To Hoe.*
- Patience - *The Irideus,* Grizzly Peak Fly Fishers Newsletter.
- Simple Song - *Poetry Depth Quarterly.*
- Softer Now - *On-line periodic letteR* - Poetic Matrix Press.
- Summer Rain - *Artscan,* Art Council Of The Napa Valley.
- The Outhouse - *Working Hard For The Money,* Bottom Dog Press.
- The Dancer - *The Gathering 7,* Ina Coolbrith Circle.
- The River's Song - *Out Of Line.*
- The Song - *Song Of The San Joaquin.*
- Variations In Red - *Flicker to Flame,* Grand Prize Winner for Poetry - Los Positas College Anthology 2005.
- Where Lichen Remembers - *Hard Row To How; On-line periodic letteR 2* - Poetic Matrix Press.
- Where The River Meets The Sea - *Hard Row To Hoe.*
- Winter hungry eyes - *Brevities.*
- When I Am An Old Woman - *On-Line periodic letteR 2* - Poetic Matrix Press; *Every First Tuesday Anthology* from Rock and Feather Press.

Content

This book is dedicated to the 'Old Men' and those who know and acknowledge the honor that goes with that title. It is also dedicated to my mother, Betty Jane Robinson Stillwell, for allowing my heart to be native, and to the memory of my father, Eugene Wesley Stillwell, a man who knew what it meant to be called 'The Old Man'.

In A Dress

Made Of Butterflies

From Breath

I sit, still myself,
quiet the heart, find silence,
breath becomes poems

Where The River Meets The Sea
For David

My father and his father
were of the sea
it coursed through
their veins.
Their eyes were the color
of the Pacific
just before a storm,
the color of the distant fog
that cooled their bodies,
but not their hearts
where their passions lived.

My mother and her mother
were of the river
they spoke the language
of the salmon,
loved round river stones
and dark quiet places
where river orchids bloom.
They saw the magic,
the significance
of the water dog
and they were colored
like the Earth
in all of its pivoting seasons.

I am of the sea.
I am of the river.
I am a combination of the two,
an estuary,
where the salty sea
meets the sweet water of the river,
where herons and egrets
congregate,
where the peaceful marsh
waits patiently
for the arrival of each new dawn.
I am of the sea and the river.
I am of the Earth.

At The Edge Of Cedar Creek With 'The Old Man'

I think often of that place,
almost an island,
with Cedar Creek
rolling gracefully around the edges
singing songs of travel,
always moving toward the sea.

I close my eyes
and my mind erases those decades
since we stood, my son,
at the edge of Cedar Creek.

There you were,
a young man,
holding a salmon,
speaking to your Grandfather,
'The Old Man'.
Your trophy silver
as dew in the cold white morning.

Excitement danced
in your eyes, and in his,
it was a beautiful fish,
but, then aren't they all?

Somewhere distant a horn sounds
time rushes back
and I find myself standing
on the asphalt of a tree lined city street
thinking of 'The Old Man',
thinking of you.

Those were happier times,
before time scattered us like wind blown leaves,
leaving only memories of that place
with its creek, its salmon
and the one we called
'The Old Man'.

How Can I Call You Dead

You come to me
in plumes of cedar smoke
curled and blue.

I chance upon your smile
in the deep yellow bowl
of the squash blossom.

Your laughter echoes
in the crystal voice of the brook
and in the song of autumn's wren.

Watching the sunflower
hold tight to the earth
I remember your hands.

How can I call you dead
when my heartbeat echoes
the rhythms of your life?

I tell myself it's temporary
and like January's daffodil
you're hiding just beneath the soil.

Great Grandmother

She called him
'Old Man'.
             To him she was simply
                      'Old Woman'.

Never
did it matter where she sat,
any place
became a place of honor.

Little girls
          gathered at her feet.

Grandmother
to grandmothers,
she was the eldest of the elders.

The old man said
she liked to face East at dawn
but he like to face West
so he could watch
the sun rise in her eyes.

When she left us
to follow the ancestors,
             poppies sprouted up
where once there had been
only rock and clay.

Great Grandfather said
poppies grew in her foot prints
lest we forget
one who loved to walk among us.

About Jim Eagle Heart's Flute

He says he found it in a dream
        the big bear flute
inlaid with turquoise and shell.

Found it in a dream
and crafted it right the first time.

No mistakes...
just right the first time.

He found it in a dream
        the big bear flute
inlaid with turquoise and shell.

Each morning he goes outside
to give thanks and greet the dawn.

The morning after,
big bear tracks circled his house
circled so as not to unwind the dream.

He says he found it in a dream
        the big bear flute
inlaid with turquoise and shell.

Found it in a dream
and got it right the first time.

Like Petals On Snow

beneath cherry trees
scattered like petals on snow
my winter haiku

Late In The Afternoon

This day colored like doves
whispers of wind
and half-hearted rain
        as clouds begin to weep.

Golden grass gone grey
waits to be born again
at the edge
        of a deer trail.

I believe myself
alone
until I feel
        the sting of nettle,
the thorny prick
of wild rose
stabbing at my legs
        cold air warm blood,
Osprey above.

With sudden silver splash
a steel head
moves up the falls
        unfettered   free!

There is only the sound
of water pounding
on rock below.
        It is a song of travel.

My eyes follow
to where fractured light
takes on the rainbow colors
of the fish.

        Osprey leads me home.
I go   having seen
what I came for
        the steel head
returning   to spawn.

Softer Now

I tell myself, be open as wind
access wants
fevered and dark,
        forget flight....

That something knocking against the heart
is not to be ignored, is not to be out run.

I wake from dreams of red cliffs,
        find dawn arcing across mountain tops,
where we know Earth's gentle curve,
spins and spins
with the centrifugal forces of time.

Look to the moon,
the wind,
I tell myself,
for answers to hard questions
yet to be asked.

Then go ahead,
cry above round river stones,
they've seen it all before
and know that life, coming and going
slices into the heart,
just as violet green swallows
cut so cleanly through evening's dusky beginning.

Softer now,
I offer first to myself the forgiveness
I extend to others.

Softer now I embrace my shadow,
desolate and ragged as it may be,
then silent as spilled blood
raise my arms to the sky
like they were wings waiting for wind.
The sky, the horizon are my altars
I offer them silence.

Be open, I say to myself,
always be open as wind.

A Train Travels Through His Poems

A train travels through his poems
becomes the lines
    the line breaks.

It was the sound of a train
that wrapped
around the water
that kept alive
and nurtured him
    inside the dark womb
beyond his mother's beating heart.

As a child
running through the tall golden grasses
of summer,
he glimpsed the hurried snake-like body
of a long black train
    belching plumes of blue on his horizon.

A train carried
him into war
and a train carried home
burnt and bent and broken
    bodies of friends.

As an old man
he remembers it was a train
that took his children
    to exciting distant places
with new names
hard at first to pronounce.

He sits on the porch watching as it moves
through the grey dusty dawns
of yesterday and today
and he knows,
it is a train
a train that travels
    through his poems.

Just Beyond Our Reach
For Barbara and Michael

Here
on the North Coast
we name the rocks
the giant ones that stand
thigh deep
in a swirl of saltwater
      waves pounding over
      sucking blue green currents below.

Rocks that once
were part of the continent
that stand now
      just beyond our reach
      where cormorants
come to roost
their droppings alabaster
      against rich brown wet rock.

Here
we name the rocks,
Northwest, Bridge, Elephant,
Mussel
and like the stars above
the ones the ancestors named
      these rocks
      tell us when we are home
come to mind
when we are not.

Surf Fishing

I close my eyes
and see my father,
my brother
in olive-green waders
dipping into the cold waves
of the blue-grey Pacific
     raising their nets
     pocketing their catch
all the while wearing the look
of the hunter.

Washing the surf fish
     their eggs clinging to our brown skin
red ribbons of seaweed
and round black rocks swirling
with the fish
in the same water that bore them.

Filling unpainted wooden boxes
with the clean catch
then racing back to the water's edge
for more
     as my father
the fisherman called for a bucket.

I close my eyes recall
the fresh smell of those fish,
hear them flopping in wet sand
     as they came ashore to spawn
     then hurried back to the safety
beneath the waves
breaking white on the beach.

The Outhouse
For Grandpa Hiram

On summer days
tourists in Bermuda shorts would stop
to tell us that our 'outhouse'
was on fire.

The 'Old Man'
would smile his toothless smile
and explain
as he sat atop his five-gallon bucket
mending the A-frame nets he sold and rented,
that "Oh no", we had indoor plumbing.

It was only the smokehouse
where he smoked until bronze,
his little fish.

Then he would sell some fish
to those tourists,
their money warm in his pockets.

The following summer those same folks
would find their way back
to the little blue house
where the 'Old Man' sat on his bucket
smoking Pall Mall's without filters
mending his nets.

There in the background
was the smokehouse
gently puffing out white smoke below its eves
scenting the neighborhood
with the sweet unmistakable smell
of smouldering alder wood
and brown sugar.

Without Song

With a voice like Raven
I do not sing,
       nor does he.

It's better that way
and since the man with the music
left in search of himself,
there is little song in my life.

      Today I stand
at the edge of the mountain I love
and watch Raven
black against a forget-me-not blue sky
fly upward like an arrow
shot through the long opalescent day
as he practices a favorite trick.

At the top of his flight
he folds those wings of night
and falls like an obsidian star
kicked loose from the heavens
until near to a death crash
      his wings unfold
open wide,
as again he takes
to the endless sky.

It was then I heard a song
so clear and melodic
a breath might have shattered it
and as soon as I realized
it was my voice
      it was gone.

Without song I watch as Raven
trickster of old
      outwits death
one acrobatic feat at a time
believing all the while
that one day I will open wide my mouth
and find again my song.

Part Of The Circle

There are simple truths
out here
on the edge of the mountain I love.

The ones with many legs
        scurry here
        scurry there
their lives are just as important
a mine.

The ones with beautiful fur
and the birds with feathers
        made of magic,
the fish with rainbows in their scales
they too
        are part of the circle.

Men cannot build spider webs
        or ant hills
             but insist
on tearing them down.

Sometimes it seems
the simpler the truth
        the harder it is to see.

But out here
on the edge of this mountain,
where wind lifts hawk high above Earth
reminders abound,
tell-tale signs
        that men are only men
only a part of the circle.

Listening With Coyote

Wary...
Coyote walks the edge
of the round Earth,
        looks in from the outside
at the bright circle of light
radiating from the naked yellow bulb
that illuminates my porch.

He knows hunger,
hears the thunder of elk and buffalo
        racing through the past
and he knows to fear
what is not free.

Wary...
Coyote walks the edge
of the round earth
        paying close attention
        to the smallest of details.

I too am wary
aching for peace.
I hear drums beating
        rising up from the past
        and in looking back
have learned to fear like coyote
those who will take from me
in democracy's name
my freedom.

Waiting

Quiet and calming
grey green olive trees
stand with me in ankle deep lawn.

Attempting to absorb the peace
I find among these acres of graves
       I walk here.

Today is cold,
still   robins sit
perched at the top of marble headstones.
Doves congregate in small groups
in lines at the edge of the road
       taking their colors
       from rock.

I meander through sections
as if I am at the supermarket
      the priests are buried here,
      the nuns over there.

Common folk
scattered like bargains
      at the end of every isle.

I notice names and dates and wonder
about these people and their lives.
When I walk away,
I wonder about my own life,
I, the wife
      the mother.

It is the graves
of the nuns that most attract me,
      for their simplicity.

Their's was a narrow winding road
with few choices
      just love Him,

      obey His commands
       pray.

Now they rest
below verdant lawns
      don their bands of gold
      and keep still
their final vows of silence.

They wait for His return.
I too wait,
but for what   I'm not sure.

I shrug,
attempting to ward off the deepening cold
      hurrying all the while
      homeward.

In Shadows Of Stone

In Raven's shadow
the yellow birds of summer
sing not their sweet songs

Beyond The Blue; Beyond The Black

The teenaged girl, after being hit
on a blue-black day
by a mallard green BMW
was air born for more than 90 feet
before her broken body
with its startled lifeless eyes
crashed onto the hood
of a yellow cab
whose driver
flashed back to another blue-black time
when a bomb
exploded in an all girls school in his own Iran
and the bodies, the body parts
of teenaged girls
fell from the sky like rain.

It was under blue-black skies
that the Cabby walked across wet lawn
to stand beside the grave
as the pink casket was lowered into the ground.
As rain began to fall
the cabdriver dropped to his knees
and sobbed,
recognizing for the first time
the feeling in his stomach
was not homesickness
but instead a deep sadness for a world
that had forgotten
that every so often a child is born
to carry the light
that leads us home.

Years later
the Cabby read an old poem
about Abraham's faith in the Father,
about how the two had talked
and even as God instructed Abraham
to lay Isaac upon the altar,
to sacrifice on a blue-black day

his beloved son,
Abraham obeyed.
But in the end it was God,
God who stopped the sacrificial act.
Faith had been tested
and passed   there was no need
to kill the boy.
Again upon closing the book
tears fell from the Cabby's eyes
this time because he feared
God somehow had turned away
from the blue, the black
of an angry world
and had forgotten again and again
to stop the test.

Promises

The boy
out on the street
walks
to block out the crying,
the shouted angry words
and fists that pound
what once was love.

He promises blood shot skies,
walnut trees, stray dogs
and passing buses
that when he's a man,
he'll not beat the mother of his children,
not when he drinks too much,
not when his pockets are empty,
not when she calls him names.

But when the boy out on the street
looks into the mirrored window
of the liquor store
he sees his daddy's eyes looking back.
They are the color of root beer
flecked with fool's gold.

The boy
out on the street
walks away from his own image
promising and promising
and trying so hard to believe
in the good of a father,
in the good of himself.

Vow To Spring

Out of the north come eagles
the devil's fire erupting from their bellies.
Listening beyond the propaganda
marching and marching for peace
the vigilant vow to remember spring.

Thunder and lightening pummel
heaven and earth. Blowing hard
the icy winds of one man's war.
Democracy's autumn rushes toward its end
as fearful eyes look toward oil dark skies
and the vigilant vow to remember spring.

The acrid smell of fire burns
our crippled lungs. Our eyes weep.
Too young to unfold still damp wings
frightened fledglings jump
from the highest nests and die afraid
while the vigilant vow to remember spring.

Black smoke hovers above the wide prairie
reaching toward ebony and scarlet skies
golden strands of grain rise like breath.
An old man watches and remembers
stories of circled wagons of greed, burning still
while the vigilant vow to remember spring.

Democracy's autumn rushes toward winter,
a fact even inattentive eyes must see.
Listening beyond propaganda
the vigilant remember the color of war is blood.
Marching and marching toward peace
we vow to remember spring.

Clock

On the small table beside the bed
a clock, purchased to keep time.
Its hands move around and around
its never changing face.

It is a clever plan
the way the gears work together
turning themselves
turning themselves.

Yet this inanimate little object,
cozy as it is there beside the bed,
knows nothing of the changing seasons,
recognizes not the rising moon,
does not reflect upon the setting sun
and does nothing to calm the spirit
or scent the air.

The ancestors might have feared
this black and white device
with its phosphorescent face,
its incessant ticking
and alarming alarm.
They kept track
by measuring shadow length
by studying the position of the sun
and they pivoted with the seasons.

But, modern mankind
needs the drama preformed by this little clock.
It marks for him each second,
each minute, each hour of every single day,
helps him run
just like his clock.

Revisiting

Pulling the car over
to the dusty edge of the flat road,
I look to the horizon seeking comfort
sometimes found in pewter grey clouds
circling slow, like vultures
on those stifling still days of summer.

None.
The horizon, an empty mirror of yesterday
white sky filling eternity
with nothingness.

It is the Sabbath somewhere.
People will gather in churches
with walls the color of gold,
looking up and out stained glass windows
from the safety of old wooden pews,
polished over the decades with the backsides
of the rich and the poor.

I think of a young wife
standing in a sunshine yellow kitchen,
stretching a white dish towel across
an ivory blue bowl
filled to the top with small red strawberries.

I can smell those berries ripening,
feel their wet heat on my dry tongue,
feel their juices soak beyond my shirt,
staining ruby my skin.

There a toddler in a berry stained shirt
plays with a toy dog,
a brass turn-key spinning on its painted back,
the linoleum is old fashioned,
from the forties
it resembles an oriental rug,
except that it is cool and hard,
and waxed to a polished shine.

Before leaving behind the past,
returning to cloudless day
and hot car,
I kneel down in powdery dust
and say a little prayer
for that child and her mother
from so long ago...

Somewhere
it is the Sabbath.

Here Among The Stones

Wild onions and larkspur
grow out here among the stones,
now and then something white
catches the eye,
a skeleton at rest
where the animal within
       lay down for the last time.

The moon
casts an eerie glow upon the stones
in this little wilderness,
       this last frontier.

Yarrow stands out
catching and holding the moonlight
like unflickering lanterns.
The wind whispers of other places
as it passes unseen,
stirring the tiny hairs on my face,
       giving me chills.

I could lie down and die here,
among the stones,
another skull among the ruins,
unashamed of the company I keep,

for there is little to be ashamed of
in nature,
and one can trust the sun to rise and set
and the coolness of night to return,
doing for the soul
       what silence can do for the mind.

Yes, I could lie down and die here,
beyond the confines of a hospital
with the flesh colored walls,
here, with the spirits of the ones
that have gone on before me,
here, among songbirds and wild flowers,
       here, among the stones.

Without Fences

Winter hungry eyes
etched deep into memory
Coyote's thin face

Or So The Old Ones Say

Let's be kind to that spider
there is magic inside her,
or so the old ones say.

She's the Grandmother Weaver
and if I believe her,
she spun the first web, built the net tight,
she's the one, caught the sun
bringing day, bringing light,
into what was once and always night.

She's the Grandmother Weaver,
and if I believe her,
she wove the first cloth
before there was moth.
It's weaving she taught
and it's clothes we've got.

Lets' be kind to that spider,
there is magic inside her,
or so, the old ones say.

The old ones to you
are Cherokee and Sioux.
Grandmother Spider is old as the air,
and always, always is there.

Let's be kind to that spider,
there is magic inside her,
or so, the old ones say....

Kestrel At Dry Creek

Through a bedroom window
I watch her land on rain darkened branch,
lift warm chestnut wings
and sit flicking banded tail
before settling into a hunter's silent stance
of watchful eyes and hunched shoulders.

Still for ten minutes,
then turning once on mottled green and grey limb
looking long into my astonished eyes
before lifting into flight and out of view,
beyond the window's wooden framework.

I feel as if we've shared something secret,
like watching a stranger dress
or knowing a best friend's husband
is having an affair
with the woman who cuts his hair.

Watching still,
I see one rich brown feather
float down
across the window's transparent eye,
before disappearing into the blue and green
of an already extraordinary day.

Raven's Storm

In the shape of a pyramid,
a ray of light escapes through an opening
in the cloud cover,
allowing Raven to cast his shadow.
As an Egret
emerges from the darkness,
the Raven calls out toward the storm.
>He is answered with loud rolling thunder
>and a blinding flash of light.

Across the marsh,
entering the bay
a lone kayak,
shadow-like at first,
drifts out of the blue-grey mist,
moving closer in silence.
The Egret rises
and flies toward the ray of light
>now only a whisper
>in a day darkening with storm.

Raven calls out,
and is answered again
>with loud rolling thunder
>and another blinding flash of light.

I wonder, who, if anyone
has heard the voice
of God
or seen the light that burns
in those eyes.
As the rain begins to fall
and the kayak slips ashore
then disappears into the day,

I wonder, who,
can say with certainty
that God
>is not here today
>conversing with Raven?

Seeing Coyote

I emerge from the garden
in the half dark of a sodden December day
in time to see a late flock of geese
high above the mirrored grey of the bay.

In the peripheral I see a shadow
move out of the bull rushes
and into the open.
It is Coyote,
seen lately trotting along the trails
that caress the curve of water's edge.

No more than a silhouette
in the lost light of another day,
I cannot see his face
but I am confident that he sees all of me.

My instincts have waned,
evolved away from the basic urge to feed myself,
to survive and now are bent around a clock
that binds me to a paycheck.

His instincts are raw, real.
He follows the rules of his world,
stays on the edge of my life, lest I harm him.
He eats only that which cannot eat him.

I stare into the space where he was
wondering what it feels like to trudge through the
wet,
hungry and knowing
this is the life you've been given,
wondering, is that is so bad?
Am I so different?

I want to answer...
No, no.

Huntress

With the talons of a survivor
she pinned her prey
to the golden grass
of summer,
made clean the kill,
the deceased
a long green snake,
its length,
twice the span of her wings.

I watched her descent
from lofty heights,
felt the stirring air
as she passed,
then watched again as she rose,
flaccid snake
clutched within her talons
and then she was gone.

The only sign of struggle,
a single gold and rust feather
fluttering down from above.

The Song

High above, a bird soars
She is alone
but not lonely.

Her reflection
dances across the water
in silence.

Even still,
I know by heart
her song,
for
I have heard it
again and again.

Stand now,
with me,
on the edge
of this mountain,
watch
the bird soar.

Close your eyes,
feel
her freedom.
learn
her song.

It is the song
of the ancestors.

Golden Eagle In January

Huge against wintery blue sky,
her shadow moves,
graceful grey upon the snow.
She glides beneath
a weak and watery afternoon sun.

Warm, inside my house,
pantry full, refrigerator humming,
I watch her circle, soar above grey fields
at the wood's ragged edge.

From the cushiony comfort of my sofa,
I thumb through seed catalogues
showcasing spring and summer,
where bright flower colors adorn slick paper,
butterflies and bluebirds soar
across warm scented pages,
no antler grey fields here.

She drops to the ground behind a toyon,
its scarlet berries blaze vibrant
against calm serrated green leaves.

When she rises again,
she carries a rabbit's limp
and broken body,
whose last mistake has brought her dinner.

I continue to browse my catalogues,
wishing I could order whole gardens,
lay them out like an ornate carpet,
but my mind is on the eagle.
I am humbled in her presence,
amazed at how hard she works
and how often she comes up empty.

Today I need not worry.
Today she's eating rabbit.

The Voice

In a dream
I walked among the ancestors.
They tended their fires,
played flutes and drums,
and danced as only the elders could.

I watched as an old woman
took ashes from the fire
and spit on them.
Then rolling them
into a small ball,
which she tossed
again and again into the air.
With each toss,
the ball changed,
until it was a tiny replica
of our own Earth.
With tears in her eyes,
she handed it to me.

I held it up against the sky,
and was amazed to feel it vibrate.
It was alive!
There were tiny birds in the skies,
the blue rivers and the seas
churned with fish and water creatures,
the land itself was alive
with animals, insects and reptiles,
many of which have been extinct
for longer than I have lived.
This tiny blue and green Earth was perfect,
unblemished, it was as it had been
when the people themselves
were brand new.

I looked into the old woman's face
and heard her say,
"Go back now,

be the voice for those
who cannot speak for themselves,
and for the Earth, our Mother.
Hurry child, time passes quickly."

When I awoke,
I held in my hand a ball,
colored blue and green.
I held that tiny ball
up against the big sky,
and whispered,
"Yes grandmother.
Yes."

Grandfather, Tell Me

Grandfather
I will sit at your feet
and if you please...
Grandfather...
        tell me the stories.

Tell me of Grandmother Spider
with the magic inside her
and how she brought light
to the dark world,
        so that we could see.

Tell me of Coyote
and of the tricks he played
and how so often it all turned around
until Coyote
tricked himself.

Grandfather,
tell me of the Buffalo
their pride and power,
how they moved like a sea
        across the prairies.

Grandfather,
tell me of the Salmon,
the swimmer, that filled the rivers
and Grandfather, tell me
        how we lived with them as one.

Grandfather,
tell me of the old days,
when the Ancestors were free
and strong, their numbers great.

Please
        Grandfather, tell me...

Patience

At creek side
time's told in light and shadow.
There are no ticking clocks,
no reason to hurry,
no tardiness,
no paychecks,
no reason to go insane.

Laughing songs of water
come to rest within us
bring the anticipation,
that comes with all journeys,
new or as ancient as the river's sorcery.

The sun rises and sets
in soft pastels,
alders filter out the harsh,
eliminating the need to squint
or hide
empowering us to greet the day
with eyes open wide.

Wind whispers its gossip;
alders and ash listen
and in turn tell their own stories.
Brown and green renewal
draws us inside pacific shadows
cooling us
cooling us.

Patterns of light play our bodies
like the instrument they are,
soft and soothing as butterflies,
monarchs, black and bronze
or dragonflies in scarlet or turquoise
floating on air above quiet water
belly dancing
with their own mirrored images.

The seldom seen hermit thrush
serenades us with honeyed notes
mastering the intricate scale of song
beyond human comprehension.

Slick-sided trout ignore us.
Our breath's rise and fall
is of no use to them.
Still the trout and the heron
teach us the power of waiting.
Over and over we are taught to wait
until that thing we most desire
cannot elude our trembling grasp.

We are taught to wait
until we become
the dance, the song, the trout,
the wind, the tree ,the egret, the heron,
the story and the listener.

We become one
with the immediate world,
one with each other,
one with love.

Ode To Rain

It is rain that fills my gutters,
my rivers,
my oceans,
soothes my eyes,
with watery wonder
re-hydrates the mind
gone dry,
dormant with too much summer.

I savor the smell
of September's dust
receiving
those first fat drops of rain.

What joy to hear the message
in thunder,
see the warning in that last slanted shaft
of sunlight
escaping
through a crack
in blue black clouds
just before they close, lock,
just before the falling
of rain.

I am filled with a longing to race
towering clouds that bring
flash floods,
cloudbursts,
here
then gone
without warning
without goodbye.

Rain dances
upon the darkened street,
each droplet
catching, holding the light
until together they merge and flood,

puddle into a silvered mirror
in which the surrounding world
may view itself.

I have awakened
to the magic
of rain beating across the roof
in early morning,
a million
tiny drums
tapping out in unison
songs of life.

There is elegance
in the frosted iris leaf,
a bending grey-green sword
heavy with rain drops,
gathering,
then rolling as one
to the plant's
base,
slipping,
without hesitation
into the depth of the waiting soil.

Pleased
I have stood barefoot
in summer's golden grass,
smelled the coming rain,
seen giant drops bead up
in thirsty dust
heard the drumming,
felt the dance upon my skin
tasted for myself
the changing of the seasons
and known the euphoria
the delight that comes
to one who welcomes,
after its long absence,
rain.

Offerings

On silent silver pond
Concentric circles
Choreograph
The rain's soft delicate dance

Winter wet
We watch...

An Offering

Heavenward,
dark grey
and bright white clouds
swirl together,
dance
across forget-me-not blue skies.

Wind loosened hair
whips across my naked face.
I feel the sting
of each tiny slap.

Wild wind,
great, swirling wind,
pins the legs of my pants
to my shins.
I struggle to stay upright!

The heavens
are not angry.

This fierce display of cloud and wind,
is a celebration, an offering
to honor the changing of the seasons.

Tomorrow
is the first day of Autumn
and tonight the power that is,
this force we call nature,
rocks!

Sky, Thanksgiving Eve, 1998

Stark white
Appearing sharp and brittle,
These fish bone clouds

Spread over
A platter of sky...
The deepest blue.

With A Chance Of Rain

The practiced voice is deep and clear
as it enters the room
through the small black square
of the radio.
"Partly cloudy today,
with a chance of rain."

It's raining here.

I wonder would the story be different
if the voice had said, "Partly sunny today"?

I have recognized the glass
half full,
then knocked it over,
leaving it empty.

A naked branch of winter
stretches across your kitchen window.
It is hung with flat grey drops of rain,
except for the last one,
the one hung closest to the heart of the tree
it blazes red as the ruby
on an old queen's finger.

Somewhere there is sunshine
and that slow fat drop
has a view all its own.

The DJ moves on to announce a song
in the voice he went to school
to learn.

I listen to an instrumental version
of *Love Is Blue*
while noticing
the few leaves still on the trees
hang limp, their color rusty.
But there in the distance

a vibrant yellow leaf,
suspended just inches
from the opaque jade of swirling creek
and there, in broken reflection
a yellow light beams back
slightly distorted, but bright
as a summer butterfly.

The song ends
the voice describing traffic
is female and so much nicer.

I want that voice
and to be partly sunny,
a sparkling drop of red
with a view
of the hard to spot sun,
the only yellow leaf in the forest.

I want to be like that.

Simple Song

For Dennis

Alders
wearing the smallest new leaves of spring
stand above and beyond your house.

I think of them as sisters,
and miss them when I leave.

Nearing sleep,
I hold you across my body.

Eyes closed,
one hand cradles your head
the other rubs worry from your back.

I am the bow,
you, the violin,
your soft rhythmic breath,
my simple song.

I long to hear it before I sleep
and when I wake.

Together we rise like the moon,
my love, and set like the sun.

And all the while,
those alders stand like trusted friends
just beyond the window
just beyond your house.

A Blossom Fully Opened
For My Father

You never spoke to me of the one called God,
but I saw the light within your eyes,
and felt the warmth of love
and peace
        radiating from your touch.

You never spoke to me of the one called God,
but I saw the worn spots
on the knees of your pants,
and on the rug beside your bed,
and heard murmurings in the night
        when only you and I were awake.

You never spoke to me of the one called God.
Perhaps there are some things
better left unsaid,
things that speak for themselves,
like how we live our lives,
        or the way we treat our neighbors,

You never spoke to me of the one called God,
but then there was no need to speak,
for your truth was a blossom
        fully opened.

In Her Eyes
For My Mother

In her eyes
I find my ancestors
        the link
                that connects me with the flesh
        and the blood of my past.

In her heart,
she holds the entire family
        like an old photograph,
        in sepia tones,
    wrapped in a lavender handkerchief
    monogrammed in pastel hues
                in perfect cross stitch.
.

        In her smile
            I glimpse the goddess,
                    so quick to retreat,
                that the ancient secret
        goes again untold.

    In the mirror   I see her eyes
looking back into my own,
it is there I find
    something immortal
and something born to perish.

    In her eyes I find
past and present
        and telling sparks of the future,
        where there are no secrets
        only time and truth
unadorned and so damned pure.

It Might Be Kansas

For Christopher

The field calls to me,
I go
to find grasses laden with grain
thigh high and bending
toward fertile earth.

I lie on my back
and look up into the day,
green grass arching,
blue sky,
black raven and me,
drifting off to sleep.

The last thought
to cross my mind is one
of Dorothy and Toto
and those fragrant poppies.

I dream of yellow bricks
and flying monkeys
and shoes,
sexy in glittery red
with oh-so-thin ankle straps
and dazzling silver buckles.

I sleep
until I hear laughter,
sitting up, startled
I see only the raven
but know I've heard
the witch.

A Poem For Forrest Deaner

The yellow light of morning
finds me in the garden
      blue oaks,
      young soldiers,
      growing promises of endurance.

In these trees
with their youthful branches
raised toward the sky,

I see color
      warm as blood coursing through
veins and roots
spanning time.

Your hands
caressed this soil,
planned and re-planned
each stone, each plant,
      they are your survivors.

And in the years that follow death
ceonothus, blue eyed grass
and golden poppies
will find solace
in this little space
      that calls us ever closer.

This is your garden,
your dream...a testament to the fact,
that once in life
you placed your hands
      with gentle purpose
            upon the earth.

*Forrest Deaner was a man who dared to dream. He founded
the amazing California Native Plant Garden at
Benicia State Recreation Area.*

Keepers Of The Seed

When we plant a seed
we walk across centuries
both forward and back

When I Am An Old Woman

When I am an old woman,
no longer burdened
by the weight of youth
pressed hard against my heart.

Let me breathe in each new morning
with its subtle changing colors.
Let me watch the mountain rise
above the lavender mist
while the song of the grebe
echoes long over my life.

Let me laugh with the loon,
rise with the sun,
set like the moon,
and learn from the salmon
the long way home.

Let me absorb the colors
of the rainbow
one by one
without needing to call them my own.

Let me find joy
in the leaves of autumn
as they dance
skitter across the wide open meadow.

Let me feel pride
and hope in the robin's egg,
hear the sweetness, the love
in the song of the frog.

Let me bend with the willow
in the face of the wind
and howl with the wolf
in the light of the round yellow moon.

When I am an old woman,
let me know that should I fail to find
an after life waiting
at the jagged edge of that longest night,
that my bone and breath
will find renewal in another's life,
perhaps a tree
or a tuft of grass will take nourishment
from that which I leave behind
and in that simple act,
in that simple act
I shall live again.

Grandmother's Slippers

The rose at the back
of my house
makes the exact same sound
my grandmother's feet made
as she shuffled
her way across this worn old floor.

The bush alone
is not responsible
the wind of the west
helps I know.

Or perhaps I have forgotten
the shuffling sound she made
with her tired old feet
and those frayed black slippers.

But sometimes
when the wind stirs the bush
it seems so real
I am forced to step aside
and allow a shadow to pass
in the hall.

The Lemon And I

1.
Lemon
fits close in hand,
cold fingers wrap around.
Yes, lemon,
with its bumpy skin
and tart juicy flesh
not circular in form,
but egg shaped.
My body also
does not follow
the rules,
or fit neatly
into tidy compartments.

2.
Lemon
does not roll,
but wobbles, tumbles,
staggers, each revolution
bends towards one end
and then the other,
it does not move with finesse
it is not dainty,
nor am I.

3.
Lemon tree,
birds flock to build
in upper echelons
seek dark and protective cover
for their nested young.
Waxy leaves of deep hunter green,
a pleasure to touch,
smooth and shiny,
flowers sweet scent the lane.
The lost and the loveless
find shelter on my couch,
and I wear lemon flowers in my hair.

The Bones Dream a Dream

The bones ramble on in their creaky old way,
dreaming about a time when they'll not be needed.

It seems,
these woman's bones
so long housed inside muscle and flesh,
so long fed on blood and breath,
dream of playing
iridescent as morning dew
beneath a star speckled sky.

Yes, these bones dream
a dream of their own,
a dream
of reclining upon the coppery green landscape
not long after sunset's brassy burn,
waiting for sister moon to float goddess-like
above tree freckled hills.

The bones dream a dream
of absorbing until becoming eerie,
the yellow light of moon
and like white gardenias at dusk
they'll shine bright back into that lunar face
that so long has pulled each cycle,
month after month
around again to its beginning.

The bones dream a dream of an after life,
where they rest naked
as only bones may,
snug against cinnamon earth,
sparkling best-linen-white
seen at last...
celebrated at last!

Dry Creek Runs Wet In Winter

To stand
at her husband's kitchen sink,
there beside the hot plate,
scrubbing vegetables,
she watches and is transformed
as Dry Creek runs wet in winter.

To Stand
at her husband's kitchen sink,
crafted of white porcelain,
scrubbing the vegetables he grows,
looking out the window
she feels like she is steering a ship,
bucking the current
as Dry Creek runs wet in winter.

To stand
at her husband's kitchen sink
there, beside the hotplate,
scrubbing the vegetables he grows
as the water rages directly
toward the window,
she becomes dizzy, nauseous,
forced to move away from that view
as Dry Creek runs wet in winter.

To stand
at her husband's kitchen sink
crafted of white porcelain,
there, beside the hotplate,
scrubbing the vegetables he grows,
she watches and is transformed
as the salmon buck the current
back to their place of birth to spawn.
She wonders what it would be like
to go back home
or perhaps to spawn
as Dry Creek runs wet in winter.

Wearing A Saffron Apron

Yellow
melts into the moss
at the edge of the roof,
drips down rain gutters
and settles into daffodils
planted in the mid-forties by a housewife
wearing a saffron apron,
craving bright beauty to mirror sunlight
so often absent in times of darkness.

Yellow
was a favorite dress
and the softest sweater ever owned.

Yellow
is the pioneer violet
at the foot of the giant sequoia.
It's the lover's round moon
and the golden trail that follows
it across
wide lakes and shallow streams.

The ebony cat
is blessed with eyes bright
as headlights at night.
Let's not forget the yellow brick road
or the down of just hatched chicks.

Yellow
is canaries and buttercups,
sunflowers and squash blossoms.
Our own pears
are pollen yellow
at sweetest perfection,
so are the ribbons tied on old oak trees.

It's the "Itsy bitsy
Teeny Weeny Yellow Polka
Dot Bikini",

wild mustard flowers,
the daisy's soft center,
my father's favorite lemon pie.

Yellow
announces morning
from the tops of tall pines
as the sun rambles again over eastern hills
before settling once more on those daffodils
planted in the fall of 1944
by a sun loving woman
wearing a saffron apron.

Now I wear that apron,
crave yellow in the dark of winter
and wait for those daffodils
to come around again.

Queen Anne's Lace
(For my grandmother, Myrtle Robinson)

They crouched
silent in the dark,
away from their sleeping children,
downwind
from autumn apple trees.
Golden globes of windfalls
littered the ground.

They could smell
the cider sweet aroma of rotting Bellflowers,
feel the chill in night air,
with its whisper of something deeper than fall,
      with its whisper of winter still to come.

They knelt there,
he held steady the spot light,
while she, the better shot, gripped the rifle,
ready to take quick but certain aim,
ready to fire into the flesh
of an unsuspecting deer.

It may be that the only lace
my grandmother ever wore,
was the Queen Anne's Lace
caught in her long black hair
as she crouched in the dark orchard
with my grandfather,
listening for the crunch of apple
that would signal the light on
      and the rifle fired.

Photograph Of An Elderly Vietnamese Woman

There is beauty in age.
You wear serenity and wisdom
as others might wear a shawl.

The silk hat, no longer young,
is a possession prized
by one who has so little.

Perfect posture speaks of pride,
of discipline,
but you are humble.
Your clothes, dark and thin
cannot keep out the season's cold.

Face lowered,
eyes closed,
you are a survivor.
I see it in your ragged nails,
your rough and bruised hands.

The camera has caught light
resting on hair, hands and face,
illuminating a surprise of smooth skin
and too the sparse sparkle
of an occasional grey hair.

Except for the photographer's
well intentioned light,
the room is dark,
its windows boarded up.

The lacquered bench,
its seat etched with large dark birds,
each one perched atop a bone pyramid.
The bench,
like your life
is hard.

Yellow Queen Of The Coi
(For Moon Mama)

In bright sulphur light
I dream I am with her
in the shallows
yellow-green with algae.

Her history is a dazzling silver thread
to braid with my own
river green
and tribal brown
tasting always of fertile soil.

Her light deepens my dark
giving me wavering shadows,
I give to her dappled brilliance.

She teaches me to dance
I step like a water strider
glide with purpose
natant, I become an illusion
of opulence in copper
feather light and free.

I learn to savor her lovers,
acquire a wanton taste for brine,
Ventilate stories of her luminosity
as she kisses my fingers,
she moves beyond my dream
before disappearing one shimmering scale
at a time.

I close my eyes tight
dry to dream her again,
but she is gone,
gone
and nothing will bring her back.

The Dancer

She is a dark silhouette
against a window
awakening to soft smoky light,
I watch
as she slow dances through
the pearl grey dawn.

Her's is a dance
that began long before man
scratched his name upon the primordial rock,
long before the birth of human ritual.

Her every step an intricate part
of life's most essential tango.

She dances,
bends and slides
between lifeless bodies,
hung on strands of web,
marionettes all.
She pulls the strings
and for however brief a time
they dance.
Fascinated, mesmerized, motionless,
I watch
as she inventories her larder,
spinning her story
across the corner of a bedroom window
filling fast with morning's yellow light.

On A Clear Day

Knee deep in spring grass,
Hat, shirt, shield her from sunburn

She is cloud and tree.
She is mother.

Dead As Arthur's Tree

Far from its beloved ruffled sea
here next to the spot
where lizards come to sun themselves
a dead seagull.

There are no gnarled cypress trees
long bent in stiff and salty wind,
no frolic of white caps to dance
on agitated purple seas, not here.

Here we have an oily spot
shiny, dark, and slick
coming right behind the king of potholes
there on the old interstate.

Down the road, Uncle Arthur stands,
arms outstretched, reaching skyward
beneath a large tree so long dead,
no one remembers even its common name.

The thing about Uncle Arthur is this,
as of late, he cannot separate himself
from what is now a tree's grey skeleton.
Arthur achieves selflessness every afternoon.

Puzzled, Arthur's wife Martha stares
at the Studebaker's broken grill, she picks up
a blood stained wing feather, once soft and white
as angel wings, then she begins to cry.

Days later she confides in her sister, Ethel,
that she's worried about Arthur and that tree,
that she has dreams of joyous feathered flight
and hears the blue ocean roaring in her ears.

As a silent grey rain begins to fall
I dig with rusty spade a hole in red dust
next to the pothole at the edge of the interstate
and lay to rest a seagull dead as Arthur's tree.

Exercise Number Three
(For Cheryl Dumesnil)

A taste of ginger,
hot, sweet and healing
awakens memories forgotten
of the mean and drunken rages
of a grandmother bitter as bile,
her cold bony fingers
offering me
a cup of fragrant tea,
steaming ginger tea to ease
what she called the curse,
to ease the cramps, the nerves
of that first menstrual period.

A rainy day poet's workshop
exercise number three...
so many flavors to taste.
I closed my eyes,
savored with astonishment, the apple,
the lavish peanut butter soft and fat,
and yes, the cinnamon stick
its touch,
its aroma bringing me back to mom's kitchen.

But, it was a taste of ginger,
that brought back a slice of the past,
that exotic cup of hot tea,
that spicy sweet warm memory
this time,
without the yelling,
this time,
without the hitting.

The Fear She Honors
(For KK Burtis)

She remembers tribal men,
their long dark hair braided
in the traditional way
      of the ancestors.

She remembers those men
as they lay in mud filled ditches
stinking of vomit,
at home
      in her native Oklahoma.

She remembers those proud men
passed out in corners,
      the broken bottle at their hip.

She remembers too,
the white men
that kicked and laughed at them,
called them names,
      derogatory names, naked of honor.

Not once, in all of these years
has she raised that bottle of poison
to her lips.
It is the fear she honors.
It is the principle
      on which she stands,
because she remembers.

Testament

Blue glow,
a testament
to a new window
from which to peer beyond our little lives
into the exotic worlds
of others.
It was the fifties and early sixties
It was television.

My father's laughter
made us smile,
made us warm.
He loved cartoons, the Three Stooges,
Laurel and Hardy.

We saw the Beatles, the moon walk,
Kennedy's funeral,
with John John
saluting by the casket,
and all the days that followed
with LBJ and Ladybird
in black and white.

Scars,
not hard to find,
scary Indians
with scalps hanging from their horses,
burned houses,
dead bodies,
smoke still rising from the ruins,
captives taken away,
always
blonde women and children,
their fates
I never knew.
I was too afraid to look.

There were Mexican men
gruff and mean,
terribly frightening,

big mustaches
dark threatening eyes.
Knives and guns
hung from belts full of bullets.
White men
buried to the neck,
screamed and screamed,
begged for mercy
from hills swarming with fire ants.

In my thirties,
I began to believe
it was probably a wise decision
not to look,
although,
there were those who frowned
at my cowardice,
those who were critical
of my closed eyes.

In my forties
I stopped fearing
the stereotypical images
of dark skinned men.

Yes,
remembering
my father's laughter,
warms my heart,
brings a smile to my face,
and too, the realization
that it was not all
champagne bubbles,
it was not all *I Love Lucy*,
that even in that time of innocence
there was harm in that little box,
in that beloved little window,
in the television
my father loved so much.

At The Edge Of The Road

She carries her possessions in a bag,
a homeless woman leading her elderly dog
on a short rope at the edge of the road.
The dog is happy to walk with his mistress.
They seek shelter,
long to put off the coming night.

The usual road debris litters their way,
tire remains left in shreds,
cans bottles and all things plastic.
Hansel and Gretel had bread crumbs
to lead them home. We have litter.

In a vineyard, four vultures
peck at grassy stubble like chickens,
above them, at the edge of the road,
a single cross marks the spot where death
broke an entire family's heart.

Holy is the feeling of this blue and grey day,
dark and light, it is the Sabbath somewhere.
Ravens call out to nobody in particular,
their messages in code, kept secret from those of us
who do not speak the blue-black language of ravens.

She carries her possessions in a bag,
a homeless woman leading her elderly dog
on a short rope at the edge of the road.
The dog is happy to walk with his mistress.
They seek shelter from the night.

My Neighbor Sleeps

My neighbor sleeps.
He has no idea I stand
here in the citrus scented quiet
beneath the spreading branches
of the magnolia tree with its giant leaves
and huge waxen flowers.

He has no idea I stand
listening to the peaceful rhythmic snoring
escaping his little house
and overflowing into my back yard,
or that within the sound of his snoring,
I find the comfort I knew as a child
awake, but not alone,
in the long dark night.

He has no idea I travel
through decades into the past to listen
as my father snored his way through
the long hours of the cool night
while the peaceful Pacific beyond
my window did some snoring of its own,
as each wave rolled up
then back across the sandy beach.

He has no idea that morning
will bring the whispered complaints
of his wife telling me she is tired,
because his snoring has kept her awake.

My neighbor sleeps.
His wife has no idea
that one day, when he is gone,
she will miss that sound like no other,
and in death's aftermath,
it will be the deafening silence
that keeps her awake.

Auntie's Poem

Seated on the couch   blue and green,
light and dark   in brocade and wood,
my ears track her location,
follow the swishing whispers
of her pantyhose encased thighs
as she moves from here to there and back.

I sip dark tea from a tiny porcelain cup
but my big boned hands cannot find comfort
embracing so delicate a circumference.
I listen as again she nears the spot
where she has left me to wait
while she searches and searches again

For Fluffy, the blue eyed, soft as silk kitten
dead now for thirty-one years.

A Child Cries

Mission Indians,
Native Americans,
they built this mission
with their sweat
      and with their blood.

Today
their bones decay,
beneath the street
and in the field
      across the way.

One by one
the names are read,
the names
of the two hundred and ten
children,
buried a hundred years ago
under the uncertain skies
      of yesterday.

Looking up
I see military planes practicing
in the clear blue above.
Blinking back tears of rage
and fear,
I know the skies of today
are no more certain
than when mission bells first chimed.

Near to me,
a child of today
cries with all her heart,
as if she's known
each and every one of these children
buried here beside this mission.

As if she knows personally
the hardships, the fear
the sweat and the blood spent here
by California's first people.

Desert

There are times,
chaotic and noisy,
when I long for the peace
of Ed Abbey's desert,
with Bats swarming,
rising up and out from the mouths of caves
filling the evening sky with a frenzy
of fluttery grace.

There are times when
I want to lay my face
against the rock formations,
the arches of the desert
and feel the hard hot stone
push into my skin
leaving behind
the rough gritty impression
that only rock can make.

I want to open my eyes
to the flower of the Barrel Cactus
touch the sharp thorns
and see the glistening deep dark red
well up on my fingertips
then dry into something less glamorous.

I want to stand at the top of a high cliff
with the wind in my hair
and look down to see hawks and eagles
soar far below that place on which I stand,
with a meandering green river
moving on toward the sea.

I want to lie down in the desert's sand
leaving behind an impression of my own
to be blown away with the wind
just before the sun rises
above the sharp angular edge
of a red ridge.

I want to see cliffs,
walls, rise straight up
from the canyon floor.
I want to see wild horses,
tails held high,
race, hooves pounding the entire length
of that same canyon and back again.

I want to watch lizards
rise up and down on their arms
in an attempt to cool their bellies.
I want to stroke one of those bellies
with the tip of my index finger
feeling for myself the perfect smoothness
of a lizard's underside.

I want to sit upon a rock and drum
in perfect unison with the beating heart
of the searing desert
as it throbs with a life all its own
while seeing red from behind closed eyes
and feeling the sun warm me
like nothing else ever could.

I want to stand naked on that same red rock
arms outstretched
and feel the wind dry the salty sweat on my skin
while my bare feet connect me
to the sweet earth from which I came
and one day again shall return.

The late Edward Abbey was a fine author and anarchist who
changed forever the way I feel about nature and mankind's
interference with it. His books include, Desert Solitaire, The
Monkey Wrench Gang, Haydukes Return, Fire On The Mountain,
and many others. He is at the top my suggested reading list.

Smooth To The Touch

Recalling haiku...
    Oh! Basho's cherry blossoms!
    We found them last Spring

Summer Rain

Heaven and earth,
red!

Sky of glowing coals,
perhaps a reflection
from ancestral fires.

The welcome smell of rain
filled the air!

Naked on the porch,
arms raised
listening, listening...

Distant thunder
whispers of autumn.
yet to come.

Even before it came
I heard the song of the rain
drumming across
Summer's golden fields.

Face lifted to sky,
I stood entranced,
grateful,
as huge drops
washed another hot summer
from my thirsty brown skin.

Someday

The fence,
a broken comb
stuck in a tangle of chaotic field growth.

A spiny skeleton
driven down below the root line,
toward the Earth's core,
where inside fires burn,
molten hot.

Some summer day
I shall soften,
melt,
renouncing the damage done
and like the fence,
once heavier,
thicker,
sink into a tuft of grass
and wait,
a dead sea gull,
for the earth to swallow me
one bent and broken feather at a time.

The River's Song

Not lost, you knew
your way home
singing the songs of your ancestors.
Washing across my feet
with the same cooling,
cleansing waters that reared salmon
and polished
once angular stones
until the moon could see herself
in their smooth exteriors.
No, you were not lost,
you knew your way home.

Oh, but there were differences
when those ancestral songs
were first whispered under starry skies
with moonlight bright,
reflected again and again,
on your young unbroken waters.

The redwoods,
elders among us, are mostly gone,
taken to build fences,
houses and hot tubs,
gone their shade once given to young salmon,
gone the hiding places
no longer available to house bird or beast.

The bed in which you once frolicked
is littered with cars
and unwanted water heaters.
They block your way.
Your once sweet water
is stolen from its bed
piped miles and miles away
to irrigate over populated
valleys grown brown.
What is left is poisoned.
Grandchildren cut their feet

on your litter strewn bottom,
and pollution goes on and on
as freely you once did.
River I shall sing
with you the gentle song of the ancestors,
walk with you for a time,
praise you,
for I have been blessed
with a lifetime in your presence,
with your sweet song,
your once healing waters
washing over my feet,
while I took rest
in the cool shade of the redwood forests
standing guard at your edge.
Now dear river, we are old
and sick.
We move slowly, if at all,
and like the salmon and redwoods
we are diminished.
We are dying.

I do not fear death,
men cannot live forever,
but dear friend,
unless mistreated
rivers are immortal.
It is for you I mourn,
and for those that did not know you
when you were wild and free,
when finding your way home
was as easy as singing
the songs of your ancestors.

Earth Day 2004

He stood
feathers faded,
tattered,
his presence, one of disarray.

It was that sudden rustle
that captured my attention.
like a witch gathering close
in indignant haste her raven robes
before vanishing
beyond the fire's flickering eye.

I stopped to stare in fascination
at a sight so unexpected
at first I did not believe
what my eyes declared true.

Wings splayed, flapping
one scaly rosy pink foot planted firm
in the murky ooze left behind
as tides recede,
the other pressed firmly
against the torn flesh of his prize
the ivory beak slightly ajar
a hiss hidden, waiting within,
both eyes blazing into my own
and only silence widening between us.

All around
children busied themselves
picking up litter,
while beneath
the deep green of arching willow
an ebony vulture abandoned the usual carrion
to perch atop a salmon
fresh from a night of high water,
its orange flesh flashing psychedelic
from shadowy underbrush.

I gathered close my feelings
like one gathering laundry
I said not a word but moved away
like a child having seen
something secret.

When A River Dies

Life congregates
at the river's wavering edge.

The living gather there to drink
that which is so precious
they would perish with out it.

I give myself to the river
believe in her magic
her mystery.

It is there,
I look for inspiration,
find whole words
among smooth stones.

It is there I feel her song
move across my skin,
enter my bones,
clear my head of tired thoughts,
cool and cleanse my body.

Rivers are the veins,
the arteries of the Earth.

Of this poem,
you need remember only this:
When a river dies...
She does not die alone.

Eclipse

A lunar eclipse,
Earth's own shadow covering
her round yellow moon.

In the dark distance,
listen, the soothing sweet sound
of an old man's flute.

Where Lichen Remembers

Kestrel and northern harrier hunt here
seeking riches found in marshlands.

I walk inside a pair of ruts
left behind by heavy vehicles
in times too wet,
flanked by antique farm equipment
and barbed wire,
marking into memory
another time.

The wire's barbs rest
like insignificant brown birds
across this rusty stretch of mineral.

A fire, in all its fury moved through here once
signing its name on the hand hewn posts
of a mostly missing fence.

A ranching family labored here,
worked hard, died young,
leaving everywhere
the tools of their trade and time,
along with their graves.

But what I came to see lies beyond all of this,
beyond the mauve skeletons
of last year's yellow star thistle,
beyond the colonies of red-winged black birds,
beyond the checker bloom
waving lavender pink striated petals
in cool westerly wind.

I came to see the grinding rock
where lichen remembers
as women sat in golden sunshine
grinding into meal acorns,
leaving in the bedrock
holes to tell at least a part of their story.

Women rested here,
grinding, nursing brown skinned babies,
gossiping across white stone,
while all around
wild radish bloomed
in rainbow colors,
each flower a cross,
each petal
the shape of a woman's heart.

Variations In Red

1.

In the voices of the old ones
I have heard it whispered
how the creator,
after finding himself lonely,
knelt upon the almighty earth
and scooped into his sturdy hands
red clay.

He shaped and reshaped it
until he found it perfect.
Then, holding his new creation
close to his heart
he breathed life and love into it.

2.

First my eyes,
and then my feet are drawn
to the flowered field
in which our children play
a robust game of untamed animals
racing across the bronze plains of Africa.

As I run shrieking wild,
unencumbered with our thundering offspring,
the old story again comes true
and suddenly I know
we are all variations of red,
variations
of clay.

Intonations

This evening's air smells
of burning wax and feathers
perhaps it's not the refineries
sneaking something lethal into our lungs,
but a lingering memory of Icarus and his story
who like many of us learned late to heed a parent's
warning.

I cannot say I listened either,
until sometime in my forties
when I heard the words of my parents
spewing easily from my mouth
in my voice,
which had somehow changed
into a voice all knowing and powerful
and yet, I heard another voice too,
the distant voice of a teenager lamenting
that she would NEVER be so bossy,
so unbending when she had children of her own.

Yeah.

Well this evening's air does reek
of burning wax and feathers
and more than likely, it is the refineries.
And the fact that I haven't heard
in a while from my child,
simply means he is busy.

The uneasiness building
inside the part of me I call the mother,
can be attributed to the fact that I too,
despite all the promises,
have indeed,
made him a victim of genetic intonations,
and like most things genetic,
he too, will pass it on
and one day when his children warrant it,
he will hear for himself as my words emerge
from his mouth
and then he too will understand
how these things happen.

Toward The End

On dusty bookshelves
poems rest in closed books, wait,
like birds, wings folded

The Swimmer

I walk the creek today,
go beyond the dam where I usually stop.
The deep hole is empty
void of salmon.

Traveling toward the upper hole,
I see a single dead fish,
one body trapped beneath a mossy log.
I free it,
not from death,
but from the obstacles that hold it captive.
I watch as it floats
like the dead salmon it is,
down stream
tail toward the sea.

I wish for them, the salmon,
the swimmers, as the old ones called them,
rivers without fishermen,
without traps and unpassable shallow places,
without culverts, rafts or boats,
only clean, cold water
moving along as it was intended.

Creeping carefully toward the upper hole,
so deep and dark,
I stop often,
standing still in silence,
so as not to frighten them.
They are here,
four of them
swimming round and round
inside the deep pool.
Backing away slowly,
I leave them in peace.

On my journey down stream,
I imagine these fish, their populations huge,
as the natives knew them,
as I never will.

They spawn and die.
It's a fact of life,
but, even in their spent and rotted corpses,
there is something magic,
something metaphorical in their ritual,
their driving need to survive.

At the dam, more fish,
all dark, all large.

I look to the sky and whisper,
"Please, Grandfather,
let them swim freely,
spare them
from the indelible stain of extinction
moving,
for the swimmer,
the salmon,
always and ever closer".

Egret

Sun
glinting

Off
alabaster
wings.

A
fantasy

Unfurling
in flight

Rising above
viridian stream

Leaving behind
reflection

Ghost-like
puff of
grace

Soft as white smoke
rising.

There Is Truth

There is truth and freedom in wind
as it blows across the earth
stirring dust into swirling devils,
rising up, then settling
on the leaves of madrone
and bay trees.
There is truth in wind and dust.

The white tailed kite will pause,
hover above fields gone
golden with summer.
The tiny shrew will hide in shadow
shivering with terror,
his fate is fate and nothing more.
Fear is truth.
It's cause is often false.

The rattlesnake will expand
his head and shake his tail,
warning the rabbit
not to venture too close.
The rabbit will listen
because the snake speaks the truth.

I will travel through my day
like all the rest.
Sweat will run down my face
sting my eyes and become
trapped between my breasts.
Sweat is nothing, if not truth.

I am honored to take my place
among nature's free,
with the wind and the dust
that covers thirsty trees,
and the shrew and the snake
in the fields and forests
where we make our homes.
In the dry heat
of a summer's day there is truth.

I awake in the night,
warm in my bed,
bone weary and tired.
Owls call out again and again.
They speak of truth
they speak of freedom
and my chest tightens
because I know,
without truth
freedom cannot be.

After Your Death

Like trains,

And wind blown clouds,
Big puffy white ones,

Papa,

That's how I see you

Just moving on,
A happy dog at your heels,

Hitching up your pants
As you go.

When It's Over

When death opens wide its door
and I step ever so lightly inside,
I want to ride high on the wings of the wind
and dance with the old ones.

Is it not the spirit freed my love,
that dances best?

Today
vultures circle
on violet blue winds
trailing across endless sky,
a swirling scarf,
it's colors bruised.

I wonder about
those nonchalant birds of death.
Do they hunger?

When I no longer need my body,
place it soft
against the earth.

When that day comes,
kiss me one last time
then give those dark birds of chance
reason to celebrate.

Let them feast my love.
Oh! Let them feast!

In A Dress Made Of Butterflies

In a dress made of butterflies
you dance at dawn
to a melody rich
with the voice of a dove,
or is it an old man's flute?

The song
declares your life perennial,
infinite, eternal.

As the sun begins to rise
and the moon slips away,
the sky grows dark with wild geese
winging their way
from cold, clear ponds
to fields full of ripening grain.
When they pass
the day is filled with the golden
yellow of a new morning,
and all the while you dance,
feet moving faster and faster,
your movements governed
by joy.

You dance on and on,
until, with a sudden and final twirl,
you stop.
The butterflies
that make up your dress,
fly away in the sunlit day,
and there you stand, head bowed,
so innocent
that I am sure you do not know
you are naked.

I move silently away
so as not to disturb your peace,
your prayer,
confident I will again watch you
dance at dawn
in a dress made of butterflies.

About The Author

I am a wild flower transplanted in full bloom from the Mendocino Coast to the inlands of California. I wilted some in the heat, but recovered enough to discover the joys of middle age. I am a descendant of the Karuk People of Northern California. My Grandmothers ventured from their brown eyed suitors to settle with husbands with beautiful sea green and sky blue eyes, hence only my heart is truly native. I carry a small grudge aimed at my Grandmothers to this day.

I find inspiration in life, nature and the culture of my ancestors. I am employed by the California Department of Parks and Recreation which keeps me close to nature. Life comes naturally and the culture of the old ones is an integral part of who I am. Poetry is my drug of choice, but it has not always been so. I find bitter sweet joy in being part of a volunteer teaching team at a rehabilitation facility in Fairfield, California. My students are in recovery for drug, alcohol and life abuses, self inflicted and otherwise.

In this first book I have tried to tell the stories of my life and the lives of others with as much truth as possible. In some cases I have failed miserably. Everyday brings a new dawn and another chance to get it right, another chance to cherish all of life's blessings, another chance to dream of and work toward peace for all of the Earth's children. - Sandy

Books from Poetic Matrix Press

Of One and Many Worlds
by Buddhist poet Rayn Roberts
ISBN 0-9714003-9-3 $15.00

Nature Journal with John Muir
edited by Bonnie Johanna Gisel
ISBN 0-9714003-7-7, hardcover $20.00
ISBN 0-9714003-5-0, paperback $16.00

The Lost Pilgrimage Poems
A book of Poetry by Joseph D. Milosch
ISBN 0-9714003-8-5 $15.00

Winds of Change/Vientos de Cambio
bilingual poems Tomás Gayton
ISBN 0-9714003-6-9 $15.00

Change (will do you good)
by poet Gail Rudd Entrekin
ISBN 0-9714003-4-2 $15.00

Merge with the river
by Yosemite poet James downs
ISBN 0-9714003-2-6 $14.00

Driven into the Shade
by Brandon Cesmat
Winner of the 2003 San Diego Book Award for Poetry
ISBN 0-9714003-3-4 $14.00

dark hills and wild mountains
poems by john
ISBN 0-9714003-0-X $14.00

Solstice
by Kathryn Kruger
ISBN 0-9714003-1-8 $7.00

CPSIA information can be obtained
at www.ICGtesting.com
Printed in the USA
FSOW02n0919160217
30719FS